Original title:
Tulip Tales

Copyright © 2025 Creative Arts Management OÜ
All rights reserved.

Author: George Mercer
ISBN HARDBACK: 978-1-80566-658-5
ISBN PAPERBACK: 978-1-80566-943-2

Conversations in a Sea of Flowers

In the garden where laughter sways,
Petals gossip in sunny rays.
A daffodil spills secrets bold,
While daisies blush, their stories told.

Bumblebees join in with a hum,
Sipping nectar, they've got the drum.
"Did you hear about the lazy rose?"
It snoozes all day, nobody knows!

The sunflowers stretch, reaching high,
"Can you believe she's scared of the sky?"
Lilies laugh, swaying to the beat,
While tulips dance on their little feet!

When the whimsical wind starts to blow,
It tickles petals, setting them aglow.
"Who made this mess?" a buttercup cries,
"Come on, everyone, it's time for goodbyes!"

Alchemy of Color

In the garden, bright and bold,
Colors whisper secrets untold.
Yellow winks, while red turns shy,
The blue ones giggle as they fly.

Green grass giggles, sways in delight,
As bees buzz by, all taking flight.
A rainbow painted, just for fun,
In this garden, there's no need to run.

Gardens of Memory

Memories bloom, just like the flowers,
Tickling thoughts in sunny hours.
The daisies tease, the roses pout,
What's that smell? A sprout's loud shout!

A squirrel twirls, a little dance,
While worms plot their own romance.
Each petal holds a laugh or two,
In gardens where the wild ones grew.

Nature's Tapestry

Nature weaves, with a playful hand,
A silly quilt across the land.
Stitches of green with patches of red,
Fluffy clouds like marshmallow spread.

A butterfly sketching a doodly line,
While ants march off, bickering fine.
Every scene's a playful jest,
In this tapestry, we're all guests.

The World in Full Bloom

The world's a stage for floral cheer,
With blossoms that dance, quite sincere.
Pansies chuckle, daisies cheer,
While violets plot to disappear!

The sun spills gold on petals bright,
As shadows stretch in the fading light.
Every bloom a comic tale,
In this garden, laughter prevails.

An Ode to Flora

In the garden where colors collide,
The blossoms giggle, no need to hide.
With petals like hats, they dance in a row,
While bees come buzzing, putting on a show.

The daisies whisper, 'Oh, what a day!'
They giggle at tulips who joined the ballet.
A daffodil winks, wearing shades of bright gold,
In this floral party, laughter unfolds.

Garden of Reflections

Mirror, mirror, in the pond,
Reflecting blooms, so brightly donned.
The roses pout when caught in a glare,
While lilies chuckle without a care.

The sunflowers turn, seeking the light,
Swaying and laughing, oh what a sight!
With leafy pals cracking jokes in the breeze,
In this garden, laughter flows with ease.

The Dance of Petals

Watch the petals swirl and spin,
With butterfly friends, let the fun begin!
A poppy tumbles, full of delight,
While violets giggle, all dressed up bright.

The breeze plays music, a whimsical tune,
As flowers hop happily beneath the moon.
Even weeds join in, with their raggedy flair,
In this merry dance, joy's everywhere!

Blooming in Silence

In the quiet of dawn, a giggle you find,
A blossom is teasing, oh so unkind!
With petals all prim in their morning attire,
They plot with the snails, making mischief conspire.

The shy little buds, peeking out soon,
Trade stories with shadows beneath the moon.
"Why bloom too loud?" said the wise old fern,
"Let the laughter of silence be what we learn."

The Palette of Nature's Canvas

In a garden where colors do clash,
Petals dance in a vibrant splash.
Red wears orange, a silly sight,
While purple whispers, 'Let's start a fight!'

Sunflowers grin, feeling quite tall,
Daisies giggle, refusing to fall.
'We're the stars!' they boldly proclaim,
While roses blush, and then feel the shame.

Songs of Blooms and Boughs

Bees buzzing tunes, a concert at noon,
Squirrels join in, a comical tune.
'Flap your wings!' cries a nearby bird,
'Let's wow the world, spread the word!'

Blossoms sway like they're on a spree,
Waving at branches, oh what glee!
With every gust of wind, they prance,
In nature's show, they all take a chance.

Stories on the Wind of Blossoms

Here flies a dandelion with great pride,
Whispers of tales from the wind beside.
Telling of picnics and cakes so sweet,
And all the critters who danced on their feet!

Each petal has secrets, oh what delight!
They giggle and chat through day and night.
A breeze carries laughter, such joyous sound,
As flowers share tales that know no bound.

A Tapestry of Floral Memories

A patchwork quilt of memories dear,
Where flowers gossip far and near.
'Remember the day we bloomed at dawn?'
'Oh yes! And the butterfly who didn't yawn!'

Pansies chuckle, making quite a fuss,
As a curious snail rides on the bus.
'Flower power,' they say, in a wide embrace,
Creating a world that's a funny place.

The Heroines of Spring

In the garden, they dance with glee,
Petals swirling in a joyful spree.
Clad in colors bright and bold,
They whisper secrets, untold and old.

A bee buzzes by, gives a cheeky wink,
"Careful now, don't spill your drink!"
As raindrops giggle and flowers sway,
The heroines shrug, 'We'll shine anyway!'

With playful bows and flirty tones,
They steal the sun, claim it as their own.
With a cheeky giggle, they flaunt the air,
"Watch out world, we're beyond compare!"

So let the blooms rise, let laughter reign,
Each colorful bloom, a voice, a refrain.
Spring's heroines in a vibrant mix,
Crafting joy from nature's tricks.

In Bloom We Trust

In a patch of sunshine, things get silly,
Flowers wearing hats, oh what a frilly!
Bouncing blossoms sing their tune,
Underneath the glow of the balloon.

Where petals dance and leaves play cards,
A garden party, no need for guards.
With a pinch of this and a sprinkle of that,
They bake up mischief, just like a cat.

Silly stems twist and shout with glee,
As friends tease each, 'You can't catch me!'
The wind joins in, spins a tight twirl,
As flowers giggle, they give it a whirl.

In bloom we trust, with laughter loud,
Each bloom a cheer to the springtime crowd.
So come and join, don't miss the fun,
In this crazy garden, there's room for everyone!

Paintbrush of Nature

With a flip of green and a dash of blue,
Nature's artists create a skew.
Swirling splashes, brushstrokes wide,
Every bloom now has its pride.

Each daisy giggles, each rose does spin,
With jokes of colors and where they've been.
"Excuse me, who splattered paint on my face?"
Comes the call from the sunflower's base.

Dandelion fuzz floats in the air,
Daring the clouds to make them a pair.
Canvases wild with laughter and cheer,
Nature's art show, the blooms all appear.

They showcase their hues, from bright to pale,
With petals and giggles, they never fail.
The paintbrush of nature, oh what a sight,
Creating joy morning to night.

Blossoms and Stories

Amidst the foliage, tales emerge,
A story of blooms, watch them surge!
Their laughter echoes on the breeze,
While butterflies join with utmost ease.

"Once upon a time, I was shy as a bud,"
Said the peony, muddy from the flood.
"I cracked my shell, got bold one day,
Danced in the sun, and found my sway!"

Lilies chimed in, with tales to tell,
"We've seen the world, oh, it's quite swell!"
With petals that sparkle, they share and jest,
Creating stories, favors confessed.

So gather around, let humor bloom,
In the garden of giggles, dispelling gloom.
Each blossom a chapter, laughter in store,
Together forever, who could want more?

The Garden's Secret Symphony

In the garden, whispers play,
Bees dance lightly, on their way.
Flowers giggle, petals swirl,
Nature's secret, unfurls a twirl.

Grasshoppers tune their chirpy song,
While worms wiggle, not shy for long.
Sunbeam's laughter, bright and loud,
Turns the shy buds into a crowd.

Blooms Beneath the Moonlight

Under the moon, daisies wink,
While crickets gather for a drink.
Lilies laugh and twirl about,
What a party, there's no doubt!

Fireflies glow, they light the scene,
Flowers blush, they look so keen.
Stars above, they join the fun,
A floral frolic, just begun!

Fragments of Color in the Breeze

Colors collide, a playful spree,
Petals flutter, wild and free.
Pansies prank in sunny cheer,
While marigolds chase every deer.

Wind teases, whispers get loud,
Every bloom tries to stand proud.
Cacti chuckle, feeling spry,
As their neighbors just pass by.

The Tulip's Timekeeper

Tick-tock goes the flower clock,
Time to dance, the tulips mock.
With every hour, they sway and shake,
Bursting with joy, for laughter's sake.

Sunny mornings make them grin,
While raindrops sing, they know they win.
Evening comes, they bow so low,
Dream of antics in twilight's glow.

The Cherished Bud

In a garden where laughter grows,
Petals dance, striking funny poses.
With a wink and a twirl so spry,
Even the roots burst out with a sigh.

Bees buzz with a giggling tune,
Tickling blooms beneath the moon.
Colors clash in a riotous show,
As garden gnomes start to steal the glow.

Worms wear hats made of soft moss,
Comparing style, they're the boss.
A ladybug struts with flair and pride,
While daisies roll, trying to hide.

But the cherished bud just holds its ground,
With humor sown all around.
It chuckles softly, unaware of the fun,
In the party of petals, it's the number one!

In the Shade of Bloom

Under the canopy, shadows play,
Where flowers doubt the sun's bright ray.
A daisy cracks a joke, oh so sly,
While violets giggle, wanting to fly.

The sunflowers nod with solemn grace,
But behind those smiles, mischief takes place.
They toss their seeds like confetti in air,
Watching the breeze take them here and there.

A bumblebee snickers, lost in the fray,
As petals flutter, eager to sway.
"Is that a bloom or a hat for a bear?"
Leaves shake with laughter, what a grand affair!

In the shade of blooms, all worries dissolve,
Their silly antics make problems resolve.
Amongst the colors, humor thrives loud,
In this floral arena, they're all quite proud.

Vibrant Reveries

A garden dreams in hues so bright,
Where colors clash in pure delight.
Petals converse in whispers and giggles,
As butterflies perform their little wriggles.

Amidst the flora, secrets are spun,
While bumblebees race just for fun.
A peony prances, thinking it's grand,
As tulips roll, trying to make a stand.

With every breeze, the flowers laugh,
Telling tales of a leafy giraffe.
The daisies joke, "What's the time, dear?
It's always the right time for a flower cheer!"

In vibrant reveries, joy blooms wide,
With petals that sparkle, and secrets that hide.
So come take a seat, here's a smile just for you,
In this garden so lively, there's always fun to pursue!

Beyond the Flora

Wander beyond the floral delight,
Where whimsy dances in the moonlight.
Petals gossip with a cheeky flair,
While critters scheme without a care.

A rogue butterfly, full of pranks,
Paints the roses in the riverbanks.
Laughing faces, both small and grand,
Gather to witness this silly land.

The trees whisper jokes with the breeze,
As dandelions roll, doing as they please.
Dewdrops titter, sparkling in mirth,
Creating gabble, a raucous rebirth.

Beyond the flora, joy spins around,
With laughter and love in every sound.
In this wild garden, just take a glance,
And find humor in every blooming chance!

Dances Among Stems

In the garden, flowers waltz,
Bouncing lightly, no one faults.
Bees are buzzing with delight,
The sun shines down, oh what a sight!

Worms wear hats, the ants wear shoes,
A party starts, nobody snooze.
Dandelions spin like tops,
While laughter echoes—never stops!

Buds become the dancing crew,
Everyone joins in, even dew.
Petals twirl and sway with glee,
A funny show for all to see.

Tickled stems that sway and bend,
Whispers shared, no need to mend.
Garden's joy, a sight to claim,
In this wild and blooming game!

Beauty in the Blossom

Petals giggle in the breeze,
Tickled pink from sunlit tease.
Bees don bow ties, very slick,
Chasing shadows, oh so quick.

Beetles boast of shiny shells,
Trading tales of garden spells.
Blossoms blush, their colors bright,
Swaying softly, quite a sight!

A butterfly, in style, lands,
Stealing laughs with flapping hands.
Every bloom has tales to weave,
In this bloom where we believe.

Jokes in colors, blooms renowned,
In the laughter, joy is found.
Petal pals, all sing along,
Their funny tunes, a garden song!

A Symphony of Colors

In a canvas of pure delight,
Colors splash, a cheery sight.
Reds that giggle, yellows hum,
A funny tune, oh here they come!

Greens jump high, in joyful leaps,
While orange grins, and purple peeps.
Each hue plays a silly game,
In this garden, none are tame.

A rainbow dance, led by blue,
Swirling, twirling, just for you.
Nature's palette, oh so bold,
With funny tales, forever told.

Harmony of laugh and cheer,
Petals bursting, drawing near.
In every hue, good vibes unite,
A vibrant tale of pure delight!

Enchanted Gardens

In a garden, magic flows,
Where every flower tickles toes.
Wands of grass, they wave hello,
Watch them dance and steal the show!

Gnomes in hats, oh what a sight,
Spinning tales under moonlight.
Roses laugh, their fragrance sweet,
While daisies tap their sunny feet.

Each petal shares a secret cheer,
In this kingdom, fun is near.
Fairies giggle, sprinkle light,
Creating joy that feels just right.

With every bloom, a jest is spun,
In echoing laughter, we are one.
Enchanted smiles, forever shine,
In this garden where hearts entwine!

The Language of Colorful Cups

In a garden bright, cups stand tall,
Color chatter echoes, a floral ball.
Red one talks back, with a cheeky grin,
While yellow spills secrets, let the fun begin!

Blue cups gossip, green ones tweet,
Petals wave like dancers, oh, what a treat!
A cup fell over, made a splash so grand,
Laughter erupts from this gleeful band!

Pink ones tease, 'Who's the best dresser?'
'I'm the sunshine,' says orange, a true confessor.
Amidst this chatter, colors unite,
In this joyful garden, everything's a delight!

Each cup has a tale, each petal a rhyme,
In this colorful realm, they frolic through time.
Sip the laughter, taste the cheer,
In the language of colors, all hearts persevere.

Secrets Woven in Silken Stems

Underneath the sun, secrets take flight,
Silken stems whisper, from morning to night.
One flower giggles, 'I've got a crush!'
Another blushes red, oh what a rush!

In the breeze, they sway, twist and twirl,
Gossiping petals begin to unfurl.
'Did you hear what Lily said last week?'
Came the hushed tones, as they played hide and seek.

'Sway with me, Daisy, let's dance around!'
They twirled and laughed, sweet blossoms unbound.
While the stems shared hugs, in the summer's glow,
Secrets of flowers continued to flow!

Beneath the chaos, joy finds its place,
In this giggling garden, there's always grace.
Walk softly, dear friend, let the laughter blend,
In secrets of flowers, fun has no end!

The Art of Petaled Reverie

In a world of petals, dreams take wing,
Each blossom creates, its own little fling.
Here comes the star, an elegant bloom,
Painting the air with delightful perfume.

A butterfly flirts, jumps from one to the next,
"Oh, what a dandy!" the blossoms exclaim, vexed.
Petals burst forth with a giggling spree,
In a colorful ballet, wild and free!

Chasing the sunlight, they twist and they spin,
"I just told a joke!" roars the bold marigold grin.
A snapdragon quips, with a bold, hearty laugh,
"Oh darling, you're just a floral paragraph!"

They dance through the day with mischief in mind,
Each whispering petal, a playful find.
In this artful reverie, joy's the best charm,
In a garden of giggles, all hold you warm.

Vibrant Chants of Flora

In the morning light, blooms begin to sing,
Their vibrant chants, oh what joy they bring!
A chorus of colors, in rhythm they play,
Plant gossip in harmony, brightening the day.

Purple pipes up, "I heard a tall tale!"
While orange erupts with a gleeful wail.
"Did you see the bee?" chirped the sweet bluebell,
As blossoms erupted, casting a spell.

In this laughing meadow, silliness reigns,
Every petal a note, every stem contains.
Hummingbirds join, with their dance and delight,
As the flowers all giggle in the warm, golden light.

Underneath the brightness, laughter does bloom,
With vibrant chants of flora, there's never gloom.
In this wild symphony, enjoy every line,
Grab a mug of cheer, and let's all dine!

Garden Mysteries

In the garden, gnomes lurch,
Their secrets in a playful search.
Flowers giggle, shake and sway,
Hiding jokes in bright bouquet.

Bees tell tales of nectar sweet,
But buzz about on tiny feet.
Rabbits dance in dandelion hats,
While sneaky squirrels steal the rats.

Sunflowers gossip, tall and proud,
About the clouds that promised loud.
Caterpillars sport their stripes,
Thinking they're the coolest types.

A worm dons glasses, quite the sight,
Says, "We dig life with all our might!"
In this plot of greens and hues,
Secrets bloom with every bruise.

The Brightest Bloom

In the garden, a flower chose,
To wear bright yellow like a pose.
She said, "Look here, I'm full of cheer!"
And danced around the bugs so near.

A bee, confused by all the light,
Buzzed loudly, gave her quite a fright.
"Dear bloom, your shade's a bit too bright,
I'm here to work, not lose my sight!"

A race began with petals flying,
As ladybugs were gently sighing.
"No matter who becomes the best,
It's all in fun; we're not distressed!"

So flowers laughed, and petals tripped,
In jokes of shyness, petals slipped.
The brightest bloom just waved her hand,
With every giggle, life was grand.

Lens of the Gardener

Through the lens, the gardener spies,
A beetle donning clever guise.
"What's this?" she asks with a grin,
"Is that a bug or just a spin?"

With every sprout, a tale unfolds,
Of sneaky vines and tales retold.
Butterflies wearing fancy cloaks,
Turning all the blooms to jokes.

A watering can with chatty spout,
Speaks loudly, wishing to shout out.
"I sprinkle dreams, I'm quite the friend,
Let's laugh together, blend, and mend!"

Every weed, with messy roots,
Hides stories of forgotten hoots.
In this garden, life's no chore,
With laughter growing more and more.

Whispers in the Wind

Listen close, the petals hum,
As breezes bring a playful drum.
"What's this noise?" the daisies say,
"Is it the sun, or mere cliché?"

The daffodils nod, all aglow,
"Let's gossip 'bout the seeds we sow."
With every breeze, a rumor flies,
Flowers plotting under sunny skies.

A robin chirps, he gets the scoop,
On a snail race within the loop.
"Who's the fastest? Place your bets!
While slugs just ponder their regrets."

In every corner, laughter sways,
As nature plays its joyful plays.
Whispers in the warm, soft wind,
A garden where the fun won't end.

Morning Dew and Floral Dreams

In the morning light they dance,
Little petals in their stance,
Winking at the rising sun,
Playing tricks, oh what fun!

Bumblebees in bowler hats,
Sipping nectar, oh dear chaps,
Stumbling on their way to work,
Chasing dreams, they never lurk.

The grass giggles, can't be still,
As ladybugs dance at will,
Worms wear shades, looking so fine,
In this garden, all align.

And when the sun waves goodbye,
Petals yawn, a sleepy sigh,
Under stars, they twirl and spin,
In the night, the fun begins!

Blooms in the Gentle Breeze

Blossoms sway like dancers free,
Laughing in the warm, soft breeze,
Petal hats and pollen ties,
Chasing butterflies that fly.

Daisies argue who's the best,
Roses claim they pass the test,
Sunflowers tower, feeling grand,
In this floral wonderland.

Dandelions with cheeky grins,
Blow their seeds, let chaos spin,
Tickling noses everywhere,
Nature's jesters, with a flair.

As day slips softly into night,
They hold a party, what a sight,
Petals twinkling, stars above,
In the garden, laughs and love!

Colors That Bring Souls to Life

Crimson blooms and golden rays,
Fill the world with bright displays,
Each hue laughs with merry cheer,
   Making dull days disappear.

Violets whisper sweet little jokes,
While lilacs giggle with the folks,
   Sunset glories paint the sky,
A rainbow laughs as it drifts by.

Marigolds wear pants of green,
Strutting like they own the scene,
Pansies wink and share a wink,
In this garden, thoughts don't sink.

As the moon begins to rise,
They toss confetti to the skies,
Colorful dreams in every sight,
Bringing joy with pure delight!

Secrets Hidden in Leafy Shadows

In the depths where sunlight weaves,
Little secrets kissed by leaves,
Whispers that the blooms will share,
Stories tangled in the air.

Caterpillars tell of dreams,
Of climbing high on leafy seams,
While crickets laugh a lively tune,
Underneath the watchful moon.

Fungi wear their dearest hats,
Inviting all the curious cats,
Roots are gossiping with glee,
In the shadows, wild and free.

When the night brings starry light,
These secrets dance out pure and bright,
Nature's laughter, soft yet bold,
In leafy corners, tales unfold!

Garden Promenade

In the garden, colors clash,
Flowers dance, a funny flash.
Bees buzz loud, but don't you fret,
They wear stripes like a tiny pet.

The daisies giggle, swaying slow,
Roses pout, with attitude to show.
Forget-me-nots whisper secrets close,
While sunflowers wiggle, oh so gross.

Chickens gossip with a squeaky voice,
While rabbits hop and leap with poise.
A parade of petals, what a sight,
Even bugs in tuxedos, well polite.

But watch out! A breeze blows wide,
Petals pirouette, a wild ride.
Gardeners laugh, and so they should,
Nature's laughter, it's all quite good.

From Bud to Blossom

In the morning light, buds peek out,
Like shy children, filled with doubt.
They stretch and yawn, then laugh aloud,
"Look at us, we're bursting proud!"

A worm below whispers a joke,
While ladybugs take up the poke.
"Why did the bloom cross the way?"
"Because it heard it's a sunny day!"

Awkward stems start their grand climb,
Blushing petals, oh so sublime.
Each flower's tale, a funny twist,
An awkward dance that none could resist.

From bud to bloom, oh what a show,
Nature's humor in the flow.
They spread their laughs, in hues so bold,
With every color, a story told.

A Ballet of Colors

A dance of colors, oh what a sight!
Petals twirl, they take flight.
Daffodils leap with a cheerful shout,
While violets wobble, dancing about.

The tulips think they're prima donnas,
"Look at us, we're the big-time winners!"
But pansies chuckle, with a wink,
"Hey, do you smell? It's time to stink!"

Marigolds cheer, their jokes are bright,
Sunflowers bow, showing off their height.
Each bloom prances, in hilarious grace,
A ballet of colors, an uproarious space.

As petals fall, they still keep the jest,
Gracing the ground, it's nature's quest.
With every flurry, laughter grows,
In this colorful ballet, anything goes!

Whirlwind of Petals

A gusty wind starts the fun,
Petals whirl like they've just begun.
Laughing flowers take to the air,
Spinning, twirling, without a care.

"Catch me if you can!" a daisy shouts,
As it dances round without any doubts.
A butterfly trips, then starts to glide,
In this chaos, it's hard to hide.

Laughter erupts from each leafy friend,
A whirlpool of colors that seems to blend.
Bees are buzzing, in hot pursuit,
Chasing petals, what a hoot!

As the wind settles, a gentle tease,
They land again, with graceful ease.
In this whirlwind, joy's the thread,
Nature's giggles dance overhead.

A Dance Among the Blossoms

In a garden where flowers boast,
A daffodil tried to learn to coast.
It wobbled and bobbed with a giggling flair,
Pretending to be a ballerina in mid-air.

A bee buzzed by with a cheeky grin,
Laughing out loud, "What a spin!"
The tulips just swayed, casting glances askew,
While the daisies joined in, creating a brew.

A caterpillar chuckled, so round and so shy,
"Dance with me now, come give it a try!"
But the daffodil tripped, oh, what a fall,
Yet everyone laughed, it inspired them all.

And so in the garden, joy came alive,
With laughter and blooms, the bugs took a dive.
They twirled and they leaped like a whimsical show,
In the dance of the blossoms, joy continued to grow.

Scented Stories from the Soil

In the soil, whispers tickle the air,
A worm called Fred sings without any care.
He tells of adventures with plants so grand,
While giggling to roots that dig through the land.

"Oh, the daisies danced while I took a nap,
They pranced like stars beneath nature's cap!"
The daisies just chuckled, waving in glee,
"We're the best dancers, come see us, whee!"

A sunflower popped up, tall and so bright,
"Fred, you should stand for a wormy delight!"
"But I'm much too grounded," Fred said with a sigh,
"Just a shy little wiggle when giggles float by."

But the tales of the soil brought laughter and cheer,
As stories went round among roots far and near.
With friendships that flourish deep down in the clay,
They bloomed into laughter, come join in the play!

Bright Horizons of Floral Voices

In the patch where blooms chatter and cheer,
A rose told a tale, "Oh, gather near!"
"Once I had dreams of a grand bouquet,
But I tripped on a leaf—what a wild display!"

The violets chimed in, "We saw it unfold!
You nearly coaxed laughter from the marigold!"
They all burst in giggles, petals all aflutter,
As the lilacs laughed, "Oh, what a clutter!"

Then a dainty pink petal declared with a grin,
"Life's better in color where jokes never thin!"
From morning to dusk, the garden did bloom,
With flowers exchanging each story and loom.

They spoke of the sun and the breeze's sweet tease,
Of buzzing bees plotting whimsical schemes.
With every sweet word, joy danced in their hearts,
In the bright horizons, where humor imparts.

Echoes of Spring's Embrace

Amidst the blossoms, a lilac was bold,
Singing echoes of spring, tales to be told.
It spoke of a bee who wore funny shoes,
Who danced through the air, doing what it would choose.

"Oh, the gardener laughed at his small, silly tricks,
As he swirled through the petals, dodged raindrops like flicks!"
The tulips all snickered, swaying so free,
Imagining all of the comical spree.

A bumblebee buzzed with a wink and a spin,
"Let's all join together, let the fun begin!"
And petals exploded in colors so bright,
With laughter as rays of a sunny delight.

At dusk, when the garden wrapped up for the night,
The echoes of giggles floated light as a flight.
In spring's sweet embrace, where the joy bounces high,
Each petal held secrets beneath the vast sky.

The Silence of the Vase

In a quiet room sits a vase,
With flowers that dance, oh what a grace!
But who knew they'd plot a floral spree,
Turning my home into a bee's jubilee?

Each petal whispers a secret plan,
To hold a party where no one can.
Yet guests arrive, all quite confused,
Wondering why the daisies are used!

A rose in a hat, quite the sight,
Joking with lilies 'til late at night.
The sun peeks in, the party's loud,
And the vase just blushes under a crowd!

In the end, with the night drawing near,
The flowers hum tunes, sticking to cheer.
When morning comes, all are asleep,
But that vase just smiles and starts to peep!

Echoes of the Wildflower

In a field where laughter grows,
Wildflowers giggle, striking poses.
Each bloom a joker, each stem a clown,
Making the meadow their lively town.

A daisy quips, 'I'm the star today!'
While bluebells sway in a blue ballet.
"Let's start a race!" a poppy shouts,
Chasing after bees with silly pouts.

The sun looks down, chuckling in glee,
At wildflowers dancing freely, you see.
Grasshoppers join, adding to the scene,
An orchestra formed in colors so green!

As dusk settles down, the laughter fades,
Flowers tuck in, each one cascades.
They dream of pranks in a world so bright,
Echoes of giggles, still heard at night!

Symphonies of Scent

In a garden where fragrances bloom,
A symphony plays, dispelling gloom.
Each petal a note, each leaf a beat,
Making the breezes dance on their feet.

Roses croon with a soft perfume,
While lilacs add a whimsical room.
The air is filled with a sweet delight,
As daisies hum tunes into the night.

But oh! The tulips start to tease,
Belting out notes that are sure to please.
A chorus forms in comical cheer,
Making the critters all gather near.

As the stars twinkle, the scents unite,
Creating a melody, pure and bright.
In the garden, the laughter flows,
With symphonies of scents that everyone knows!

A Canvas of Color

Brush strokes of petals, a vibrant scene,
Nature's own artist, with colors so keen.
A canvas spread wide, with blooms all around,
Sprinkling laughter from the ground.

Crimson and yellow, like rainbows on high,
Where butterflies flit, and the bumblebees fly.
With every hue, a tale comes alive,
In this lively gallery where dreams survive.

A green leaf giggles, making a quip,
As purple pansies do a little flip.
The tulips don hats, painting a scene,
With laughter echoing, serene and keen.

Each sunrise brings new shades to behold,
A hilarious masterpiece, vibrant and bold.
In this garden, the colors are free,
Creating a wonderland, wild and zany!

Petals in the Breeze

Petals dance in the sunny air,
A cheeky bloom without a care.
They twist and twirl, a merry crew,
Waving hats, like flowers do.

Bumblebees buzz with glee and cheer,
As if to say, "Come join us here!"
A daisy trips and falls on ground,
While laughing daisies gather 'round.

Butterflies giggle, chasing tails,
Wings coated thick with sweet details.
The tulips gossip, sharing tea,
"Did you see the bees? They're so zany!"

With every gust, a silly game,
Petals shout out their blooms' names.
In nature's party, all are free,
What a sight! Come laugh with me!

Whispered Blooms

In a garden where secrets float,
Blooms gather 'round in a flower boat.
Roses tell tales that make them blush,
While tulips giggle and start to hush.

They whisper low like gentle breeze,
Spilling funnies that tickle knees.
"Why did the flower cross the street?"
"To get to the garden, life is sweet!"

Daisies wink with a cheeky grin,
"Come sit with me, join in the din!"
The violets nod, so wise and sly,
As petals chuckle and drift on by.

Under the sun, they plot and scheme,
Blossoms dance in a bright daydream.
In their world, laughter is gold,
Whispered blooms never grow old!

Colors of Dawn

With the sun peeking, the petals glow,
Colors of dawn put on a show.
A red one shouts, "Look at me shine!"
While yellow yells, "That's my line!"

Bluebells giggle as they sway,
"We'll steal the spotlight today!"
Each flower bursts with vibrant glee,
In this daily spree, wild and free.

Orange pops like a joke unplanned,
As laughter blooms all over the land.
Pinks tease greens, "You can't catch us!"
While violets giggle, causing a fuss.

As the colors blend in the sky,
Our plant pals wonder, "Oh my, oh my!"
With every sunrise, fun's reset,
In nature's palette, you'll never fret!

Secrets Beneath the Soil

Under the ground, they whisper tales,
Of tickets sold on rooty trails.
"Did you know?" a seedling ponders,
"Last night's party left folks in wonders!"

Nuts and bulbs exchange a grin,
While digging worms join in the din.
"Why is the dirt so soft and fun?"
"Because of all the parties run!"

All the critters, a hidden show,
Organizing the underground flow.
With carrots packing a tiny lunch,
Potatoes join, ready to munch.

Beneath the surface, friendships grow,
Where roots mingle in a secret flow.
In this world, laughter and clay,
The buried giggles will never sway!

The Scent of Stories

In a garden full of jest,
Stories bloom from east to west.
Petals giggle with delight,
As the bees take flight in sight.

Sunlight dances on the green,
Tickling blooms, a vibrant scene.
Wisdom wrapped in fragrant cheer,
Laughter blossoms, loud and clear.

Each flower tells a silly tale,
Of comical winds and whimsical gale.
In laughter's shades, scents intertwine,
As we sip tea with the sunshine.

So join me now, come take a whiff,
Of stories sweet, like candy mist.
With a giggle and a cheer,
Let's find the joy that's hiding here.

Wind's Brush on Bloom

A breeze tiptoes through the dress,
Of petals blushing in finesse.
Whispers float, they tease and twirl,
Gentle jests in floral swirl.

"Hey there, bee! Come dance with me!"
Said the flower, with glee, you see.
But the bee just rolled his eyes,
And hummed along, beneath the skies.

Wind laughs loud, a playful jest,
Ruffling blooms, giving them rest.
"Catch me if you can!" they say,
As they sway in a frolic play.

With each petal's quirky prance,
Nature joins in a joyful dance.
Laughter rustles through the leaves,
In this world where fun believes.

In the Realm of Flowers

In a meadow of vibrant hues,
The daisies gossip and amuse.
"Did you hear about the rose?
She threw petals on the toes!"

A daffodil chuckles out loud,
While the violets gather 'round.
"Oh dear, what a clumsy sight!
Rolling petals, what a fright!"

The sun is smirking, hanging high,
As butterflies flit and fly.
"I'll paint the skies with laughter bright,
In this garden of pure delight!"

So come and stroll through this spree,
Where blooms behave so whimsically.
Each blossom has a tale to spin,
Let's join the fun, let laughter win!

Petals of Whispered Dreams

In soft whispers, blooms confide,
Of silly wishes and dreams wide.
"Wish you were a bumblebee?"
They chuckle softly, full of glee.

"Does this dress make me look bright?"
As petals giggle in the light.
"Let's prank the gardener!" they say,
Hiding tools, mischief on display.

Chasing shadows, teasing the sun,
In the realm where flowers run.
With every flutter, laughter soars,
As petals dance through open doors.

So pour a cup of nature's brew,
And let the flowers talk to you.
In their world, joy blooms supreme,
In petals of whispered dreams.

Chronicles of the Colorful Fields

In fields where colors clash and play,
The flowers dance in bright array.
A daffodil wore shades of red,
While violets argued, mischief widespread.

The bees were buzzing, plotting pranks,
Stealing nectar, forming ranks.
But daisies giggled, quite aware,
Of bees in capes, acting debonair.

Butterflies donned hats from leaves,
Claiming sunshine, oh, what thieves!
Lemonade served in petals wide,
As tulips looked on, full of pride.

In this garden of laughter and cheer,
Silly antics, we hold dear.
A dash of joy, a sprinkle of fun,
In every bloom, the laughter won.

Garden of Echoing Laughter

In a garden where jokes do grow,
Laughter sprouts, putting on a show.
Funny faces in each flower's glare,
Tulips giggle at the squirrels' flair.

Petunias whisper secrets too,
While roses blush with wild, bright hue.
Joking violets tease the breeze,
Tickling everyone with such ease.

Sunbeams play hide and seek again,
Making shadows of the garden's kin.
With giggles echoing, round they twirl,
As daisies spin in a frolic swirl.

So come and join this merry scene,
Where every flower's humor is keen.
In the blooms, find your own delight,
And leave your worries, take flight!

The Heartbeat of Spring Gardens

In springtime's pulse, the pranks begin,
With flowers wearing grins, a playful spin.
The tulips feign to tiptoe late,
As daffodils claim, 'We're awfully great!'

A hummingbird competes with the bumblebee,
In a race for nectar, both wild and free.
Sunflowers laugh, they're quite astute,
Counting all the critters in pursuit.

Frogs croak jokes from their leafy thrones,
While ladybugs roll on little stones.
Pansies chuckle at the sky so blue,
And every flower joins the fun crew.

So listen close, let nature's giggle,
Remind us all to jump and wiggle.
In every bloom, a silly spark,
In spring's warm heart, a joyful lark.

Whispers from Petal-Laden Paths

On petal paths where secrets hum,
A wind of jokes swirls, oh so fun!
Tulips play tag with clouds above,
While daisies dance, wrapped in love.

Beetles host a comedy show,
As butterflies flutter to and fro.
Wildflowers share their tales of old,
With punchlines found in petals bold.

In this scented realm, where giggles soar,
Every color whispers, 'Tell us more!'
Larks join in, adding harmony,
Creating a symphony of jubilee.

With each step down the winding lane,
You'll find laughter eases the strain.
So stop and listen, let your heart sway,
In gardens where humor finds its way.

A Garden's Symphony

In a garden of giggles, a saxophone plays,
The daisies are dancing in whimsical ways.
A chorus of crickets, a laugh here and there,
As the sun sets behind, with a golden flair.

The roses tell jokes that are charmingly bright,
While the peonies twirl in the soft twilight.
The lilies are chatting, sipping sweet dew,
And the friendly old oak joins the fun too.

A sunflower winks at the butterfly fleet,
While the violets chuckle, oh, what a treat!
The melody grows as the night takes its hold,
In this garden of laughter, where stories are told.

With a fanfare of colors, the moon gleams so clear,
As the flowers serenade all those who draw near.
In the symphony splendid, where joy takes the lead,
Every bloom holds a note, in this floral creed.

The Language of Flowers

In the meadow's embrace, the flowers conspire,
To tell secret stories, their language inspires.
The daisies, so cheeky, make quite the display,
While the daisies express, 'Don't be so cliché!'

The poppies are gossiping, sharing a brew,
While the lilacs insist, 'What's new with you?'
The blooms form a union, a club so bizarre,
Debating about who's the prettiest star.

With petals of laughter, they chuckle and play,
Their puns full of fragrance, brightening the day.
In this vibrant confab, each bloom has its say,
Deciding if fern should join in or stay away.

As the wind whispers secrets to blossoms unbound,
The flowers unite in a chorus profound.
In the garden so merry, with smiles we adore,
Each sprout holds the secrets of bloom folklore.

Blossoms in the Moonlight

The garden awakes in the soft silver glow,
Where giggling buds sway, putting on a show.
Under moonlight's laughter, a carnival blooms,
In the night air, echoing fun, joy resumes.

The petals are bouncing, like kids at play,
While the daffodils leap, 'Let's dance the night away!'
With skirts of bright colors that shimmer and sway,
In this festival of flowers, who needs a bouquet?

The nighttime reveals all the capers and schemes,
As the blooms share their folly, wrapped up in dreams.
Tulips recount tales of their quirks and quirks,
While nightingale whispers give each stem some perks.

With the stars as confetti, the moon as our guide,
The blossoms create magic, in laughter they glide.
As the night slowly fades, and dawn starts to creep,
The garden's sweet giggles will linger, not sleep.

Vivid Hues of Spring

In the palette of spring, colors burst into cheer,
With violets quipping, 'Did you see Frank's rear?'
The zinnias giggle, sporting hats so grand,
While the peonies gossip, their petals all fanned.

The azaleas prance, with a rhythm so bright,
Swaying to the tunes spun by bees in flight.
'Oranges are silly; look at their stance!'
As they whirl and twirl, in a bright flower dance.

With vibrancy reigning, each bloom takes a turn,
The tulips are laughing, oh, they really can learn!
Secretly plotting, a prank on the sun,
To hide behind clouds, just to have some fun.

In the garden alive, where humor ignites,
Every blooming buddy has its quirks and delights.
As the springtime unfolds, with colors that sing,
Together we grow in this festive time ring.

Elegance on Stem

A flower wearing a big, fine hat,
It wobbles, and oh, how it sat!
A dance with the breeze, such a sight,
Yet trips on a bee—oh, what a fright!

With roots that wiggle in soil so deep,
They gossip at night while the whole world sleeps.
Laughing at daisies, they think they're so cute,
But wait till the rain, when they all get the boot!

Petals like skirts that twirl in delight,
Who knew a bloom could throw such a fright?
With every gust, it holds on real tight,
Nature's own dancing queen, what a sight!

In gardens they strut, all colors in line,
But just one misstep, and it's tumble time!
For in the grand stage of the flower show,
Even the poshest can take a hard blow!

Stories from the Meadow

In a meadow where flowers like chatter and boast,
A daisy declares it's the best on the coast.
But the roses all laugh, and the poppies just giggle,
For they know the truth can make daisies wiggle!

A sunflower claimed it could reach for the sun,
But tripped on a vine just for fun.
"Oh no!" it yelled, "Help with my hair!"
As petals flew high, floating up in the air!

In the whispers of grass, the tales take a twist,
A butterfly's secret that just can't be missed.
It once met a beetle who thought he could fly,
But flopped on a leaf with a loud, carefree sigh!

Each blossom and bug, in wild laughter's realm,
Turns the 'serious' nature into a comedy film.
With petals and wings, let the stories unfold,
In the meadow where life is both funny and bold!

Nature's Paintbrush

A brush made of petals, splashing with cheer,
Colors collide, oh, what do we hear?
A painter of blooms, in laughter they draft,
Each stroke with a giggle, a tickle, a laugh!

The canvas is bright, but a bumblebee flew,
It dived in the paint—now it's yellow and blue!
With stripes on its back, it zooms here and there,
"Oh dear!" it buzzes, "I'm a work of art rare!"

A tulip teases the braver delphiniums,
"Your colors are nice but you sing in the wrong tunes!"
Blossoms burst out into a silly ballet,
Each pirouette sending the pollen astray!

With each playful splash, the meadow's aglow,
As petals role-play, turning pink into show.
In Nature's grand studio, laughter fills the air,
Creating a masterpiece beyond all compare!

Beneath the Spring Canopy

Under leafy ceilings, where giggles reside,
The flowers chit-chat, they've nothing to hide.
A posy that prances, oh, what a grand glee—
Spinning around for both critters and me!

"Watch out!" yells a lily, "There's trouble ahead!"
"Is it ants? Is it rain? Or just lack of bread?"
They all stop and ponder, in serious thought,
Only to burst into laughter—oh, what a plot!

A butterfly sneezes, the daffodils hoot,
While the clover plants giggle, finding it cute.
These tales of the garden, woven with jest,
Turn every small moment into a grand fest!

And as spring unfolds with its whimsical ways,
Each flower grows playful, brightening our days.
For beneath the great dome of sky painted blue,
The laughter of blooms is the best kind of hue!

The Art of Blooming

In the garden, blooms arise,
Dancing petals, bright as pies.
A bee slips on the silky lace,
Swearing it will win the race.

The tulips shout, 'Pick me, pick me!'
While daisies laugh, 'No, let me be!'
A daffodil bursts out with cheer,
Saying, 'I'm the star of the year!'

Buds peek out with sneaky grins,
Who knew the fun that spring begins?
They play tag with the morning dew,
As clouds giggle, "What's wrong with you?"

In this patch of colorful jest,
Who knew flowers could be the best?
They prance and twirl, such a sight,
In the sunny warmth of light.

Echoes of Earth

In a field where laughter grows,
Flowers gossip, striking poses.
"Look at me!" the peonies plead,
"Oh please, we're the ones who lead!"

The roses snicker, red like wine,
"Silly daisies, you'll never shine!"
But the violets whisper low,
"Recess time, let's steal the show!"

A windy day brings silly shakes,
Leaves shout, "Help! We've lost our fakes!"
Pansies chuckle in a row,
Sipping sun like it's a flow.

With every bloom, a tale unfolds,
In pollen fights, brave hearts are bold.
Earth laughs back, it knows the fun,
In every petal, laughter's spun.

A Tapestry of Color

In gardens where the hues collide,
Flowers gather, side by side.
With orange hats and purple shoes,
They cheer for spring, a colorful ruse!

A sunflower claims to lead the way,
Bragging loudly, "I'm here to stay!"
But little buds begin to tease,
"Your sun-kissed crown is just a breeze!"

The roses throw a party grand,
With petals dancing, hand in hand.
While tulips, with their floppy grace,
Skip around, trying to embrace.

In this photo of pure delight,
With colors that are simply bright.
Each bloom bows to the spectacle's lore,
As laughter rings forevermore.

The Secret Lives of Flowers

In the midnight breeze they chatter,
Floral secrets, oh what a matter!
"Did you hear about the bee?"
"I saw him dance beneath a tree!"

The lilies giggle, petals flaring,
"Watch the daisies, their skills are daring!"
But up above, the moon just beams,
Listening close to all their dreams.

At dawn, they trade their slyest jokes,
Petunias snicker; oh, what blokes!
"Who will wear the morning dew?"
"Not me, I'd rather wear a shoe!"

In every bud, a story hides,
With whispers where the mischief bides.
Flowers frolic, life's their stage,
In their world, there's no old age!

Secrets of the Blossom

In a garden where blooms wear their hats,
A flower sneezed – it startled the cats!
They jumped and they spun, in a humorous chase,
While petals giggled all over the place.

Behind the leaves, a bee held a show,
Dancing with raindrops, putting on a glow.
"Come one, come all!" he buzzed with delight,
As flowers twirled under the moonlight.

A sunflower whispered, "I'm king for the day!"
While daisies rolled on the ground in dismay.
"Your crown is too tall!" the roses all jeered,
And the tulips just blushed, feeling quite seared.

With laughter and cheer, the blooms made a pact,
To share all their secrets and grow with the act.
In this garden, so wild, they found much to say,
About giggles and wiggles that brightened the day.

Petal-Powered Dreams

Once there was a petal, quite spry and sprightly,
Who dreamed of innovations – oh, so brightly!
He wanted to fly, to zoom through the sky,
Till a breeze came along and said, "Give it a try!"

He painted a rocket with pollen and dew,
Attached it to a leaf that was fresh and new.
"Lift off!" squeaked the rose, with her friends in a whirl,
As down came the daisies, all ready to twirl.

The rocket did wobble, it looped and it twirled,
While the petals all gasped at this magical world.
But soon their adventure turned quite a flap,
As a bee flew too close, and got stuck in the gap!

With laughter erupting, they turned around tight,
And set off for home beneath stars shining bright.
They learned that dear dreams come in all sorts of schemes,
And fun's in the journey—a petal's own dreams.

Kaleidoscope of Nature

In a garden of colors, a party took flight,
Where violets tangoed with daisies so bright.
The lilies were laughing, the sweetness on cue,
As sunflowers pranced, painting skies in pure hue.

A butterfly chuckled, snuggled in green,
While bugs played on trumpets, all shiny and keen.
The wind blew a tune that made everyone sway,
As petals all jived in this floral ballet.

An orchid complained, with a frown on her face,
"This groove isn't right; there's no style or grace!"
But as orchids do bluster, the whole crowd just grinned,
And they swayed to the rhythm, with laughter unpinned.

As the sun set the stage, in hues soft and low,
They smiled at their antics, their colorful show.
For in nature's big dance, through giggles and song,
There's joy in the chaos, where all blooms belong.

Floral Whispers

In the hush of the evening, the flowers confide,
    Whispers of laughter, secrets inside.
The lilacs are giggling, the poppies so bright,
    As the tulips roll over, melons in sight.

"Did you see how that rose tried to bloom with a flair?"
    "Her petals got tangled, she's stuck in mid-air!"
The daisies snicker, as they gather around,
    With petals all fluffed, ready to clown.

The evening grows cozy, with jokes in the breeze,
While marigolds grace us, sweet scent with such ease.
A sunflower whispers, "I dream all day long,
    Of dancing in starlight and singing a song!"

So they laugh and they rumble in this floral delight,
    Telling tales of mischief as day turns to night.
In a garden of whispers, where all dreams unfurl,
    Each petal a chapter, each bloom – a new pearl.

www.ingramcontent.com/pod-product-compliance
Lightning Source LLC
Chambersburg PA
CBHW071827160426
43209CB00003B/218